MANIFOLD MANOR

Philip Gross

Illustrated by
Chris Riddell

faber and faber
LONDON · BOSTON

22813.

First published in 1989
by Faber and Faber Limited
3 Queen Square London WC1N 3AU

Photoset by Parker Typesetting Service Leicester
Printed in Great Britain by
Richard Clay Ltd Bungay Suffolk

British Library Cataloguing in Publication Data is available.

ISBN 0 571 15405 0

Contents

Trespassers Will . . .

The sign says PRIVATE.
Tall scrolled-iron gates
are rusted shut.
Nobody comes here,
but . . .
> now and again
> was that the dull chink
> of a padlock chain?

Inside, the drive is lost
in old-man's-beard and brambles,
grass so long uncut
it might conceal a man-trap
but . . .
> crisp, clear
> as breaking glass, a child
> laughs. Can't you hear?

The trees close round
like lawyers whispering the clauses
of a long-forgotten will.
They won't tell you a thing.
But still . . .
> though no one spoke
> you feel you've come too late
> to join the joke.

[1]

Sometimes you glimpse
a gutted tower, empty windows.
Other times they fill
with odd long slants of sunset.
Still . . .

        did someone call?
        Was it a bird? Your name?
        You climb the wall.

Look. Nothing. Listen. Nothing.
Through scents of leaves and soil
here comes a sweet sharp whiff
of . . . what? You might remember
if . . .

        you find the wooden gate
        into the garden. And you wonder,
        am I late?

It's later than you can imagine.
Ease the latch. The wood is soft
with mildew though the hinge is stiff.
It crumbles in, into a sudden hush,
no *but* or *if*.

        It's what you had to do.
        This is a private party.
        They're expecting you.

The Twenty-Sixers

We are the twenty-sixers:
gypsies, jugglers, necromancers.
Hear, sir, here we come:
Fortune-tellers, cheapjack tricksters.
Cross our palm, sir. Join our dance, sir,
or we'll strike you dumb.

An Angel Arguing with an Ancient Ape . . .
A Bishop Breaking Bread with a Baboon . . .
A Carrion Crow Clad in a Crimson Cape . . .
A Doctor of Divinity who Dreams of Doom . . .

We are the twenty-sixers:
gypsies, jugglers, necromancers.
Hear, sir, here we come:
Fortune-tellers, cheapjack tricksters.
Cross our palm, sir. Join our dance, sir,
or we'll strike you dumb.

An Eccentric Earl with Eagles to Exhibit . . .
A Fund to Finance Fiends who Fail to Fall . . .
A Goblin Gabbling Grace beneath a Gibbet . . .
The Hounds of Hopelessness that Howl around the
  Hall . . .

An Intellectual Imp Inventing Interesting Ills . . .
A Jumped-up Judge who Jokes about the Jews . . .
The Kids in Khaki every Kind of Kingdom Kills . . .
Lieutenant Luck who Lends them Lives to Lose . . .

We are the twenty-sixers:
gypsies, jugglers, necromancers.
   Hear, sir, here we come:
Fortune-tellers, cheapjack tricksters.
Cross our palm, sir. Join our dance, sir,
   or we'll strike you dumb.

The Monstrous Maybes in the Mire of Might-Have-Been . . .
The Nevermores that Nag you in the Night . . .
The Odd One Out who's Only Out on Hallowe'en . . .
The Princess Pretty-Please who's Painfully Polite . . .

The Questionmark that can't Quite Quench your Quest . . .
The Ringing of a Right and Royal Rhyme . . .
The Silent Song that cannot be Suppressed . . .
The Ticks and Tocks that Take their Toll of Time . . .

We are the twenty-sixers:
gypsies, jugglers, necromancers.
   Hear, sir, here we come:
Fortune-tellers, cheapjack tricksters.
Cross our palm, sir. Join our dance, sir,
   or we'll strike you dumb.

[4]

The Undertaker's Ugly Understudy, Ulf . . .
The Violent Vicar whom his Victims Vex . . .
The Woman Who Went Walking With a Wolf . . .
The letter the unlettered sign with: X

The Youth who Yawns but Yearns to Yell out *Yes!* . . .
The Zombie with his Zip stuck in the Zoo . . .
But without a twenty-seventh we are less
than breaths of wind. So we have come for you.

We are the twenty-sixers:
gypsies, jugglers, necromancers.
Hear, sir, here we come:
Fortune-tellers, cheapjack tricksters.
Cross our palm, sir. Join our dance, sir,
or we'll strike you dumb.

Jack

There were feathers everywhere. It must have been an aviary, but every cage was wrecked, doors lolling, netting torn. And feathers, a mosaic of them, white, black, all the colours of the paintbox, everywhere. And silence. Then . . .

'I say I say I say . . .' The bird was scruffy, black, with a grey cap at a cocky angle, and a spry glint in his eye. 'You look a likely lad. Tell me: what bird works underground?'

I frowned.

'My, my,' he crowed, 'we're slow tonight. A mynah bird! Ever met a mynah? No. I knew one in the War. Name of Major Mynah . . .'

'Liar!' I butted in.

'No,' he hopped and fluttered, 'not a lyre bird. Different kind of tail. See, you can always tell a lyre. By his tale! Oh dear me, it's the way I tell them . . .'

'Stop!' I shouted. 'Where is everyone?'

'Inside.'

'And how do I get in?'

He clacked his beak: 'Depends on where you are. Where are you?'

'I was hoping you'd help me to find out.'

'Make up your mind. I thought you wanted to find IN . . .'

'No jokes,' I pleaded. 'Help me out. No, in.'

'Well, now you're asking.' He sidled a bit closer. 'Time for introductions. Tell me: what door never leads where you expect?'

'I said no more jokes!'

'No joke,' he cackled, taking flight. 'A jackdaw, silly! Follow me.'

'Where?' But he was already out of sight.

The Wind Fugue

out of the bramble-garden
(and they said I wouldn't)
onto the crumbling terrace
(and they said I didn't dare)
under the empty window-frame
(I almost thought I couldn't)
shin up slowly, squint into the darkness
(there!)

cat-foot, mind the splinters
(all the tales they told me)
broken glass and plaster
(they won't see me scared)
just an empty house now
(smells unloved and mouldy)
that's the one, the music room, the door's ajar and
(there!)

a tumble-down church organ
(was that all I came for?)
tiers of shattered keyboards
(there's a trembling in the air)
the pipes go up and up and
(no, it's me begins to quaver)
up to a broken skylight where the wind comes
(there!)

a hollow whistling hum
                    in tall pipes, just a semitone
apart, the slow
                    drones jar and blur
and fail with the wind
                    (Am I afraid? No, worse – alone
like never in my life. There's no one, nothing,
                                        there.

The organist who hymned
                    his days and nights away
alone, the wife who died,
                    the unborn heir
are nowhere. Ghosts?
                    A game for kids to play!
Imagine yourself nowhere *in the world, not here,*
                                    not there.)

Lord Boneleigh

Lord Boneleigh,
one and only

son and heir,
looks down

from his nose-in-the-air
high hall

on all
the heres and theres,

the hues and cries,
the whys and wheres,

the ratty scatty
human race,

the fuss and jostle
of the town.

His face,
set like a fossil

in a small
slit in the wall,

frowns
down.

Do you know
this poor Lord?

No? When you
are meanly bored

(so no no no
nothing will do)

and lonely
(everybody's silly

except you)
he calls:

*Come up
to my parlour of stone.*

*We'll sup a cup
of bitter tea . . .*

And curiously,
if you do

you're on your own.

The Cry-by-Night

It's wind in the eaves, they'll tell you, mice
in the attic, old timbers stretching and yawning . . .
It's no good. Hear it once, you're lost: Miss

Nobody's grieving, somewhere. How they hurt,
those hard jagged sobs. She is trying to pull
something up by the roots. Maybe her heart?

Where is she? You *must* know. Down quiet
corridors, up stairs, you follow listening
at every door, nearly there, never quite.

But where, you have to know. And who?
And why do you feel no one in this world
could comfort her but you? Because somehow

you see her, in a waterfall of hair, as pale
and thin as moonshine, with a face as clear
in your mind as its own reflection in a pool.

Is it for you she waits up, never sleeping,
Miss Wind-In-The-Eaves? No. Touch her, she'd be
gone, and leave you nothing but the weeping.

[11]

Jack's Nature Study

That bird again. He cocked his beak: 'Well? Did you find them?'

'Who?' I said.

'Why, everybody. Everybody's somewhere. If you know where to look.'

I was getting angry. 'What is this? Some kind of riddle?'

'Ah, riddles!' He hopped a few times. 'I was hoping we'd get on to riddles. Try this for a start. It's a common-or-garden word . . .'

Each of us a day –
        long wink
                back at the sun.
We fold ourselves away,
        we blush and shrink
                when he is gone.
He loves us, loves us not,
                we say . . .

That's our disguise.
        We keep our mission dark,
                transmitters tuned
east every morning; spies
        in every garden, every park;
                a network underground.
We have grass-roots support.
                Day's eyes.

In the Formal Garden

A peacock feather. And a simple stone
in the herbaceous border like a child's
first tooth, carved *BENJIE.*
EVER FAITHFUL. 1899.

And I've been here before.
A gust of dead leaves brushes by
like bustled skirts. I step aside; I know
my place: the gardener's boy

who crouches by the trellis, there,
to glimpse three lacy Misses flit and chime,
their shuttlecock hung motionless
above their heads, like time.

A spaniel pup flop-lollops at their heels.
Then that dry rustling: Lady M.
stands over me . . . Pa wrings his cap and begs:
'He's not a *bad* boy, ma'am.'

She freezes: 'If I ever catch him
looking at my gels again . . .' Unmanned,
bowed, slashing weeds, I catch the hush
of silks, and round, my billhook in my hand,

on a pinched proud face, beneath
its silly coronet. Waddling in draggled finery,
the peacock stares. It rattles up its fan
in a shivering hiss. And screams.

The sky is darkening fast. 'Get in,'
Pa calls. 'Daft ha'p'orth.' From the shed
we hear it shriek again. Pa grins,
'Like the voice of the dead!

Damned bird. I'd wring its neck.'
The first drops streak the pane.
Somewhere, a yappity panic breaks and falls
to whimpers: Benjie, left out in the rain . . .

The Chaos

(From the papers of Sir Magnus Manifold, the 13th Earl, who died without heirs, 1832.)

Estate? It is my world! God knows, I've paid,
and not only gold, for my 'sequestered grot',
my waterfall, my lake, my lovers'-knot
of paths, my Chaos: carts of quaint rocks laid
in artful confusion, for my children to parade
Romantic notions. So they did, before
one went to childbed, and the rest to war.
I live in one wing with a valet and a maid.

Leeches and lawyers bleed me. Every border
falls to rout with weeds. Rank creepers braid
the stonework. Poets scribble their cod's-rot
about the place's 'melancholy sweet disorder',
damn their eyes! Even the Chaos is decayed.
I knew its ways once, but I have forgot.

Jack's Elementary Riddles

*'OK, OK,' he said, 'I'll make it simpler. You can't get them
simpler than this. The answers, at least. The questions?
Well . . .'*

Spell what you will, my first is where it starts.
My second is who everybody claims to be.
My last's in birth and dearth but not in death.
The answer is the sum of all my parts.
     Now, take a deep breath.
          You have me.

*

My first is in rainbow and also in stew.
My second's in Heaven but not in Hell.
     My third is in the pot.
My fourth is in wives and their menfolk too.
My last's in the middle of a waterfall.
               And what
     am I? The greatest part of you.

*

My first is the direction of the rising sun
and if my first is 5, my second's 1.
My third's what makes *her* more than *he*.
My fourth's a cross that's lost its head.
In *heir*, my fifth is read, not said.
     You'll end your days in me.

*

The first of *first* is first in line.
(There's six of my second in that!)
My third is in three and four and forty.
My fourth seals the fate of the fat.
    I'm not a cold, but woe betide
    you if you've caught me.

'Is that all?' I said. He winked
'All? Absolutely. So they used to think.
More complicated now, of course, with chemistry.
Do I have to spell it out? It's elementary!'

Peter Poulter

Peter's such a *good* boy, isn't he?
'Why can't you be like Peter?'
parents tell you. Peter is exemplary.
How strange he's got no friends.
But his parents agree:
'Yes, Peter's *such* a good boy!' Only, now and then . . .

          CRASH

plates   *zing*   *through the air*

       clocks   *stop*   *glasses clatter*

         SMASH

                      (he's not to blame, his parents swear)

FLASH   *the lights fuse*   *mirrors shatter*

                           (Peter Poulter's there)

Peter's such a quiet boy. Studious.
Speaks when he's spoken to.
'He never bothers us,'
his parents say. 'We have our lives
to lead. Him? Make a fuss?
He's very grown-up for his age, I'm pleased to say.' And
   then . . .

CRASH

plates   *zing*   *through the air*

          clocks   *stop*   *glasses clatter*

          SMASH

                    (he's not to blame, his parents swear)

FLASH   *the lights fuse*   *mirrors shatter*

                              (Peter Poulter's there)

The mirror's cracked from side
to side. Peter can only stare.
In one half there's a wide-
eyed Peter, very pale. The other
shows a fiery-dark sprite-child
who bares his teeth and laughs like fury, when . . .

          CRASH

plates   *zing*   *through the air*

          clocks   *stop*   *glasses clatter*

          SMASH

                    (we're not to blame, his parents swear)

FLASH   *the lights fuse*   *mirrors shatter*

                              (Peter Poulter's there)

[20]

And is it just a shy boy's fright
that leaves him trembling? No,
no, Peter is a good boy. It's the sprite
who has to spoil things,
his parents know, 'in spite
of all we've done for him . . .

in spite of all we've done . . .
      in spite of all . . .
            in spite . . .'

      In spite.

      Hush!
Here comes Peter now
       tiptoe

      pit pat
    pitter patter
pitterpatterpitterpatter

        CRASH

            He's here.

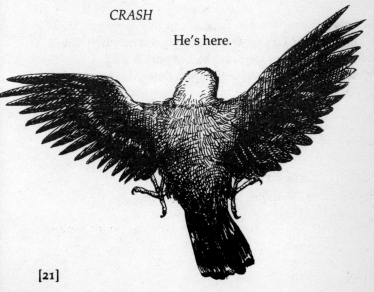

The Cat's Muse

And the fat
cat musing on the mat
sang
(flat):

I'm a tabby flabby house cat, just a fusty ball of fur,
A never-caught-a-mouse cat with a rusty sort of purr.
But sit down on the hearth mat and watch the fire with me.
I'll show you some of the dark and wild cats up my family
   tree.

        Oh I'm no common-or-garden cat.
        There's something you might miss:
        the sabre teeth that I unsheath
        when I stretch and yawn like this.

Sheba was a temple cat in Tutankhamun's days.
She had a hundred priestesses and several hundred slaves.
She curled up on an altar on a bed of purple silk,
Off saucers made of beaten gold she dined on camel's
   milk.

        Oh I'm no common-or-garden cat.
        My pedigree tends to show.
        My tail is like a cobra
        when it lashes to and fro.

Captain Moggan was a ship's cat and he sailed the Spanish
    Main.
He went all the way around Cape Horn and made it home
    again.
His claws were sharp as cutlasses. His life was sharp and
    short.
He died in Valparaiso, leaving kittens in every port.

> Oh I'm no common-or-garden cat.
> Haven't you noticed my
> one lop ear like a pirate's hat
> that flops across my eye?

Greymalkin was a black magic cat with fur as slick as pitch.
She held covens in a cavern with a wild and wicked witch.
And when she went out hunting on a moonlit winter's
    night
The village folk would bar their doors and dogs dropped
    dead with fright.

> Oh I'm no common-or-garden cat.
> Who knows what I might do?
> You'd better keep me happy
> or I'll put a spell . . .
>   . . . on . . .
>   . . . YOU!

Jack's Black Day

I'm in everybody's black books
Blackguards give me black looks

Black magic   Black arts
Blacklegs with black hearts

Blackmail me in the dark
Blacklisted   Black mark

The black sheep of the family
Black Jack that's me

Black-eyed beaten black-and-blued
Guess the colour of my mood!

                    *

Tonight, I dreamed I flew
to Africa. No moon, no star
to guide me, I flew into black,
the heart of it. I flew so far.
At dawn I dabbled in a pool

inlaid with pebbles of pure jet.
Among the cool shades of a tree
I saw the Queen of Sheba, black
and strong and smooth as ebony,
a casual hand stretched out to pet

a leashed black panther, deadly-
sleek as an underground stream.
It purred and then, like any black
cat, crossed my path. The queen
bent down to me and said . . .

>   *poor light*
>   *that has no shadow*
>   *poor white*
>   *that has no black*
>   *poor day without a night*
>   *no dreams to follow*

I preen and glisten in the sun, Black Jack.

Mrs Stoker

Deep down the back stairs
Mrs Stoker
rules the kitchen
with a red hot poker.
    Upstairs
the house sails on
like an ocean liner:
silver salvers,
fine bone china.
    Down there,
copper cauldrons
cloud the gloom.
The furnace fumes
like an engine room
    full speed ahead.
Kettles wail
like souls in limbo.
She looks on
with her arms akimbo
    and what was that she said?

fetch stoop carry girl, on yer feet and run girl
ain't put me feet up since the world begun girl
God tossed me something like a half-baked bun
    I caught it in me pan
    He says, it's called a man
so stoke up the oven girl and call me when it's done

Coals crack red
like the centre of the earth.
Over in the corner
is the bed where she gave birth
 to Jim and Jack
and Joe and Judas
and oh, how many more.
They marched off singing
to some high and mighty war
 and none came back.
She soldiered
on alone.
They say there's nothing
she can't do with a bone,
 and her bread
comes up like thunder
and her gingerbread men
stand to attention
on your plate. Only then
 do you remember what she said:

fetch stoop carry girl, on yer feet and run girl
ain't put me feet up since the world begun girl
God tossed me something like a half-baked bun
    I caught it in me pan
    He says, it's called a man
so stoke up the oven girl and call me when it's done

    Upstairs, luncheon
    is being served.
    Blood red broth
    makes a rich hors d'œuvre.
        The guests exclaim.
    The lady of the house
    goes pink with pleasure.
    The cook? Oh yes,
    she's an absolute treasure,
        Mrs What's-Her-Name . . .
    while deep down the back stairs
    deep into the night
    the black lead grate
    is banked up bright
        as the heart of the sun
    and Mrs Stoker
    watches it burn
    and dreams of the world
    being done to a turn
        and her work, shall we say, well done.

The Secret

Who am I? Have I got a name?
They won't say – not the man who comes
with the keys to walk me after dark.
    He is dumb.

Not the nurse who spoons my food.
She talks to herself, and me, sometimes,
but not what I long to know.
    She is blind.

What am I like? What is
this thing I am, that they must hide?
Listening at the bolted shutters
    I hear outside

tiny steps, tiny voices.
Am I a giant, and the rest so small?
How am I known? Nurse answers,
    if at all,

'a secret'. She says 'sir'.
She mutters on about 'the family name'
or shakes her head and tuts
    'the shame, the shame.'

On the wall a circle
shadows where a mirror might have been.
I stare at the polished table. Something
    swims in its sheen

much like the face I watch for
when I'm led out on the roof at night;
she looks down from the sky, round,
    very white.

She must be ugly too. She turns aside
for days or goes veiled, yet greets me
when she can. She is not afraid.
    She meets me

face to face. She is my one
pure light. She counts my time. How long
has it been? For ever. But for her
    I made this song:

wan face
wall eye
neither you
nor I
know where
know why
wait for me
beyond the sky

And that is our secret.

The Oubliette

The past is brambled over, smothered.
     I could have stepped
off into darkness and be lying undiscovered
     down there yet.

How long had an uneasy memory
     of it slept
beneath its grille of ferns? It glistened inwardly,
     so wet

it might have been a wishing-well
     except
no wish was granted. This was the forgetting-cell,
     the oubliette.

How long did it take them, simply
     being kept
to die? Someone, somewhere, is dying now. So easy
     to forget.

Service

For X, in service,
    probably not lovely,
        no one's daughter
            in particular,

who lost her hours
    of daylight on her knees
        to a gritstone floor,
            never raising her eyes

but to climb to an attic
    by a back stair, glad
        of a share of a mattress,
            too knackered to dream . . .

for her, and all the others,
    this:
        the old scullery floor
          is cracking up.

A flagstone
    four men could not lift
        has buckled and split.
          A hundred years

it's taken it, but look,
    a mushroom!
        Pale white skin
          as soft as yours.

This is her flesh,
     a musty taste
          of earth, but sweet.
               In memory of X . . .

take, eat.

Two Men in a Moat

The moat has drained away
        to this:
a seep of bog among the brambles
        in a ditch
except when evening breeds
        thin mist

which whitens in the moonlight.
        Then the moat
remembers something old,
        a slow
unsteady chop and drip of oars,
        a boat . . .

and two grey men, two monks, one fat,
one lanky, and a small grey cat.
 It's Friar Fulsom, Friar Faint
 and the cat, who's afraid of water.
These brothers of the simple life
are bickering like man and wife.
 It's Friar Firkin, Friar Fitch
 and the cat, who's afraid of water.
One believes in eating well.
One is afraid of mice, and Hell.
 It's Friar Forward, Friar Fret
 and the cat, who's afraid of water.
They need a cat, they both agree.
But should it be a *she* or *he*
 for Friar Fussell, Friar Fripp
 and the cat, who's afraid of water?
A tinker sold one for a groat.
He left it in a bag beside the moat
 for Friar Frogmore, Friar Frayne
 and the cat, who's afraid of water.
One says: to entertain a *she*
is against the rules of the monastery.
 It's Friar Fettle, Friar Frost
 and the cat, who's afraid of water.
One says: there's not a tom-cat yet
who grasped the meaning of 'celibate'.
 It's Friar Flambo, Friar Frail
 and the cat, who's afraid of water.
One says neutered, one says not.
Neither is quite sure which they've got.
 It's Friar Fangle, Friar Feck
 and the cat, who's afraid of water.

Eight hundred years it's been.
　　Each night
their ghosts forsake theology
　　and fight.
The boat upsets. The monks go down.
　　The cat was right.

Madame Mirador

She was almost a nun.
This dressing table was her altar
with its phials of incense
and the triptych of a mirror.

Two panes fold in
and trap you in a corridor
of glass that curves away
gently to eternity; only your

own ugly mug butts in
and blocks your view,
massed ranks of it
like warriors in a tomb.

She was too lovely to escape
men's admiration, on the stage
or in the bedroom of an earl.
This mirror was her cage.

Night after night it showed
her slightly paler, less
substantial; every time
the cutting edge of glass

would shear a near-transparent
sliver of herself away
and so she faded, growing
threadbare in the light of day.

Only a thousand ghosts of her
hunt down the long glass corridor,
identical. But every door she tries
is a mirror. Every mirror is a door.

The Poet's Prayer

The poet in the garret is
a washout in his narratives.
    His sonnet
    has a curse on it.
His bloody Border ballad
is as limp as lettuce salad.
    His sestina
    looks even greener.
His historical verse drama
creaks on like a suit of armour.
    His villanelle
    has gone to Hell.
And when his verse is free
it just goes on and on till it bumps into the end of the page
                             (you see?)

    All he can do
      is a dry
        hai-
        ku:

Lord, I want to be
disdainful of success. Please
give me chance to try!

The Ballad of Bill Beale

you know Bill Beale
him who tolls the bell
well
the tales I could tell

        big bull of a man
        he could bowl a ball
        hump barley by the bale
        but he'd brag and brawl

till he fell
for a girl did Bill
called Pearl
it boded ill

        a baleful tale
        this ne'er-do-well
        fell to burgling to bag
        a bauble for his belle

till one black day
bold Bill fell ill
with a belly ache
he bellowed for his will

        the beadle brought a Bible
        and Bill began to blub
        about the Tower Of Babel
        and Beelzebub

and the boys below
that's where I belong
Bill babbled
and my time won't be long

but just betimes
Pearl butted in
yelled *Belt up Bill*
she belaboured him

all your bullying and beefing
and your bad black bile
I've had a bellyful
then with a smile

big baby!
Bill laid his bald
head in her bulging lap
and bawled

she led him to church
belatedly
said *pull that bell*
and maybe

you'll pull the other one
if Pearl looked pale
burly Bill looked paler
at the altar rail

yes he tolled the bell
but folk still tell
of what Bill Beale
was told by his belle

ding dong
(yes it's got bells on)

What to Call a Jackdaw

sneak thief   snatch-and-grabber   artful dodger
  Jackie Braggart

cliff-cackler   folly-squatter   relic-snatcher
  back-chatter

cheeky chappie   keep-cackler   chuckle-chook
  windbagger

cock-o'-the-castle   monk's canary   glib-gob
  bluster-budgie

silly-sexton   Jack-in-the-pulpit   hop-o'-my-tomb
  flibbertigibbet

deadman's-doorman   graveyard-gossip
  sweep's-brush   sooty-bottom

scraggle-wing   petty-crow   jolly gagman
  merry-andrew

day-bat   rookster-trickster   dusk-dove
  corvus monedula

*(and out from the thicket of words hopped Jack, a bit apologetic:
'Only me!')*

The Captain's Pearls

Captain Shadrach Shaw spent much of his long life afloat in the South China Sea. He was equally at home in the spice-palaces of petty island potentates, and the huts of poor fishermen and Buddhist monks. When he returned to England at the age of eighty-two, he brought a huge trunk which, he said, contained his pearls. He lived, apparently in rags and eating little, for another twenty years. He died smiling. Only then was the sea-chest opened, and a paper, nothing but a scrap of paper, found inside . . .

This is the legacy
of Captain Shaw:

    if you would sail the sea
    that has no shore

        say only 'Yes, I see'
        and 'No, I am not sure.'

Hot Air Balloon

Here Be Dragons . . . Old maps bred them, just too far
away to catch or tame, of course. But what comes here:

over the trees with a gravelly huff, half sigh, half roar,
and a prickle of flame? I drop my book and stare

as it shoulders the sun aside. It settles, slow
as an eclipse, a candy-striped Big Top, hushed now

but for a creak of tackle, wind-hum in the wires . . .
The awning sags; its crate of precious wares,

half tiger cage, half laundry basket, thuds down,
spilling a figure out like dice across the lawn.

He finds his feet, dusts his greatcoat, wraps his scarf
twice round, squares his sideburns and his sad moustache,

and strides towards me, tipsy-brisk, as if uncertain
which of us is Stanley, which is Dr Livingstone.

He does not have to speak. I know where he has been –
over glassy deserts, jungles steaming in the sun,

peevish oceans, to the limits, to the outer regions
where the maps go blank, and men dream dragons,

anything, to fill the awful void of Do-Not-Know
that drifts in, endless, indescribable, like snow.

The Forest Children

The old macaw sat shackled to her perch. No pretty polly but a
smuggler's moll. Her tongue was made of horn.

Red, yellow, blue: a toddler could have painted her. But her eye
was a gold ring from a pirate's ear. Its centre was black, jackdaw
black. It drew me in. And this is what I saw.

Bright fathoms of leaves alive with shrieks and colours . . .
Languid spider-monkeys with the faces of philosophers

who see and speak and hear no evil . . . Deeper down
in shadow, we the children of the forest bed (known

in our own tongue simply as the People) slip by silently
as underwater, and as naked, plucking fruit from trees

as we ourselves are plucked by spirits or disease.

We laze. We swim. We play. At dusk we tip our darts
with death, ghost out to raid, and bring our foe's heart

home to eat and praise him. Snuggled in one hut like
  kittens
in a heap, we sleep, begetting dreams and children,
  children

till the big men find us, some with guns, some with
  machines
that snarl into our forest, some in black with creeds

to teach us we are evil. We escape, into their dreams.

Africa

And the swallow
dipping from the eaves
grieves:

Long times gone
I lived in a tower
under a clock
that struck the hours

Children passing
under the tree
told the time
of year by me

When the wind
brushed by I heard
under its breath
a single word

The word caught
rustling like a fire
through all the birds
along the wire

Then all at once
both near and far
it spoke inside us
– *Africa!*

Weeks out at sea
we fell to land
on pastures drowned
by drifting sand

I clutched a thorn
tree bare as bone
saw women reaping
fields of stone

A child looked up
beneath the tree
and said *What have
you brought for me?*

I could not speak
I could not stay
North! says the sun
and I obey

Year after year
to you I bring
the summer

But I do not sing

[49]

The Sage of Kitchnapur

The tiger's head yawns on the wall. A hundred years
is no time here, in the India Room. Beside the door
an elephant's foot collects umbrellas. A stuffed boar
stuck by a Bengal lancer frowns, as if he hears
        a voice say *Aaah!*
    The more the years, the less each day.
        You see? But you do not.
    The more you keep, the more it slips away.
        And you say 'What?'

Beneath the aspidistra squats an ancient man, his skin
like dried mud and a dhoti white as Himalayan snow,
so still that for a moment you think, is *he* stuffed? But no,
he greets you with an infinitely sad, wise, patient grin
        and he says *Aaah!*
    The more you hunt, the more you kill.
        You see? And you say 'Who?'
    The more you want, the less you have your will,
        Sahib, you too.

The India Room was furnished by a Colonel in the Raj.
He collected this and that, and that, and . . . He appears
to have acquired a wise man in among his souvenirs.
The Colonel's eyesight wasn't good, the sage not large.
        The voice says *Aaah!*
    The more you stare, the less you see.
        You see? And you say 'No.'
    The more you run about, the less you are free.
        And you say 'Oh.'

In Kitchnapur a scholar studied ancient script.
He found a text inscribed inside a large brass jar
and leaned in. Then the Colonel swept through the bazaar,
and bought the lot, contents and all, and had it shipped.
      The voice says *Aaah!*
The more you lose, the less you grieve.
      You see? And you say 'Eh?'
The more you stay at home, the more you leave.
      What *can* you say?

Then there were wars. The Empire shrank like pink
ice cream left in the sun. Retired, shipped home
loaded with medals and gin, the Colonel sat alone
and swore he heard a voice. Or was it just the drink
      that said *Aaah!*
The more you . . . ?
                    'No!' you say 'No more.'
      It fades away: *I know.*
My grandsons have grown old in Kitchnapur.
      It is time to go.

Spirit of the Place

Your dog's off on the track of nothing
you can see. He's ripping up the dew.
Last night's leaf-smoulder trickles on
    behind the yew.

Who is the trespasser, who the guest
no one invited, who the host?
I cannot be possessed or dispossessed.
    I am no ghost.

Lean on the door jamb. Feel the scars
of chisel and rasp. Here is a spy-slit
window on the stairs. A candle gutters
    that you never lit.

Who left a billhook by the chapel? Wings
crack the evening; rooks take fright.
A child's swing in the garden swings
    on in the night.

The manor wallows in the swell and sway
of woods and fields, an ark of stone
that drifts in silence with a freight
    no one can own.

What's gone has no voice but the whisper
of your pen. Not the girl who played
wind-music to herself, nobody's sister.
     Not the scullery maid.

Not me. I am that nothing not to be
described. You could fill a book
with the adjectives that fall from me
     like leaves. Look!
                         I am at your back.

Song of the Empty Dovecote

The savage dove
has lost her name. She goes from land to land.

                She does not understand.

The homeless dove
has been in temple courtyards, palaces and barns.

                She has watched them burn.

The blackened dove
has seen too many arks turned from too many shores.

                She has jumped borders.

The hunted dove
has learned to take her chances. She has fed on carrion.

                She is sick of good intentions.

The hawk-eyed dove
has seen through pity. She is sharpening her claws.

Last night I dreamed I saw

the savage, damaged dove.
I hardly knew her. *I am coming home*, she said.

Remember me. I was afraid.

She hunts for love.

She never said it would be easy.

The Doors

There was a boy who found himself alone
in an endless house. How had he come
there? He forgot. He wanted to go home.

But there were doors, doors, doors, a door
of each and every colour. Down each hall,
on every landing, round each corner, more.

Which way to go?
It would take him a lifetime.
But he tried the first one, so:

THE PINK DOOR

Pink powder-puffs of cherry blossom nodded in
    the windows.
On papered walls, pink piglets, shocking pink
    flamingoes,
pranced. A clinging boiled-milk-with-sugar smell.
    And first
a creaking, then a grizzling, then a cry: a small
    pink fist
thrust through pink lacy frills, punched free;
    a face
puce, puckered, mouthing Me! Me! Me!

Not this way, no, go on, go back, not here . . .

[56]

THE YELLOW DOOR

The summer blazed like footlights. Far below
    a field spread out a view
of buttercups and dandelions rampant, and a child
    he thought he knew
sat in a flattened picnic spot. Crushed stalks
    oozed bitter milk. The sun
wound up the clocks. He watched the butter-gold,
    the honey, melt and run.

Not this way, no, go on, go back, not here . . .

THE GREEN DOOR

The third was green.
A greenhouse heat
glazed all the leaves
with beads of sweat,

leaves, tattling tongues
that seemed to say
that *she* was here,
with whom? For Jealousy

the green-eyed monster
thrives on unripe grapes
and shades of lime.
Sour apples give you gripes.

Not this way, no, go on, go back, not here . . .

[57]

The next
     was red.
          The party hushed.
He stood
     in the doorway.
          Flushed
and bloodshot
     military men
          and wives
with rouged cheeks
     clutched their claret
          and their dripping knives
as if uncertain
     whether he
          was friend or foe
or food.
     He blushed:
          'Oops. Time to go!'

Not this way, no, go on, go back, not here . . .

THE BLACK DOOR

He tried the black door.
It was not a door.
It was a shadow
on the wall. His own
shadow stepped straight in.
He could not follow.

Not this way, no, go on, go back, not here . . .

THE BROWN DOOR

Surely this was the last?
    The boy stepped in
    to a brownish gloom.
The door shut with a puff of dust.

And there were books, ton on ton
    of them, piling up
    to where the ceiling
might have been, all bound in brown,

in a rich dark smell of leather
    peppered with mould.
    There was one desk,
and, cradled in a great armchair

an old old man. The boy stood
    dumb. He saw the brown
    age-speckles on the skin;
drawn tight to the ridges of the head.

[59]

He saw the white quill pen, the open
    page, the looped snail-
    trail of ink already fading
to brown, and the story, which began:

The brown door was the last.
    The boy stepped in . . .
    And again, and again.
He could not stop, the words like rust

eating the page, eating his life away.
    'What happened in the end?'
    he cried. The old man turned
and shook his head, as if to say

'No end. There is no end. And no escape.'

Not this way, no . . . But every door
was wrong. He snatched the book,
unfinished, flung it to the floor

and stopped. The pages blew and blurred
like a beating of wings
shaken free, a caged white bird

about to fly. And there
lay one white page unwritten,
open like a door . . .

. . . and he looked in.
A bare room: floorboards, echoing

white-washed plaster walls.
It was empty. There was nothing, only smells

of raw stripped wood, and paint.
The window faced him, without curtains,

only the frost of dawn
in a dazzle of cold thin winter sun

taking his breath away.
So afterwards how could he say

if this was the beginning
or the end? But he was stepping in

to somewhere high and full of light
all round him, white wings thrilling into flight.

Jack's Final Riddle

'And what about me?' said Black Jack. 'All this white *stuff. Wasn't I there too?'*

'Of course you were,' I said. 'I heard you chattering outside in the garden. And you know what?'

'Hey, I'm the one who asks the riddles! Tell me.'

'I wanted to listen. I really did. So I looked out and . . . Well, there was everything again.'

He looked bedraggled suddenly. 'Did I spoil it? Are you sad?'

'In a way. But no. I like this place. Can I stay?'

'You tell me. Make yourself at home. Oh, one last thing . . . Just to keep you going . . .'

    Everybody lives here.
        Each goes in alone.

    Some say it is nowhere,
        some, in a box of bone

    bound in the softest leather
        and only inches wide.

    You can travel for a lifetime,
        maybe more, inside.

The more you shout about it,
      the less you see and hear.

Sometimes you need darkness
      to make your vision clear.

If you don't see through my riddle
      all you have to do is look.

If you think the answer's simple,
      well . . .

you write a different book!

Tailpiece

This is not the end!

   Manifold Manor is not my private property. If you feel at home there, it is just as much yours as mine. It is big enough for you to find a room for anyone or anything you can imagine. If you want to make further discoveries, all you have to do is to write them for yourself.

   Several of the poems here are games that can be played again and again, and come out different each time. So . . .

'The Twenty-Sixers'. The possibilities are endless. Keep the refrain and invent your own verses. You can do this alone or with a group.

'The Wind Fugue'. A fugue is a cleverly patterned piece of music and some of the greatest fugues have been written for the organ. Like a fugue, this poem uses the trick of counterpoint: two different tunes are played at the same time.

'The Cry-by-Night'. What does it feel like when two words almost rhyme (mice/Miss, pool/pale), but not quite? Play two notes on the piano, a semitone apart, for the answer.

'Jack's Nature Study' is one kind of riddle. You can make a riddle about any flower, any creature, anything.

'The Chaos' is a sonnet, a very tight and tidy kind of poem, because the 13th earl would have liked the world to be like that.

'Peter Poulter'. A poltergeist (German for 'noisy spirit') is not so much a ghost as a storm of disturbing energy that seems to build up around certain places and people, often children.

'Jack's Black Day' is more than just a game with words, because in this part of the world people with pinkish-creamish skins tend to call themselves 'white', and people of all shades from coffee-cream to ebony, 'black'.

'The Secret' borrows a legend from Glamis Castle in Scotland. An heir was said to have been born monstrously deformed and kept hidden, all his long life, from the outside world.

'The Oubliette'. The French word 'oublier' means 'to forget', and an oubliette was a dungeon in which prisoners were simply left to die – one way of forgetting them. In how many countries are people still 'forgotten' like this?

'Service'. Two kinds of service are brought together here. Look up the Holy Communion in the Book of Common Prayer and see why.

'Two Men in a Moat' could have gone on for ever, if the boat had not capsized. Start making up your own names and the story will follow in its own way.

'The Poet's Prayer' mentions only a few of the possible kinds of poem. How many more can you think of?

'The Ballad of Bill Beale' shows what can happen when you take one word and squeeze it very hard. The word here is 'bell', but why not pick one for yourself? On a blank sheet of paper, write down very quickly all the words you can think of that sound like the one you chose first: then shake them about till they sort themselves out into a story.

'What to Call a Jackdaw' follows a very old poem called 'The Names of the Hare', which was a kind of charm or spell to ward off the bad luck a hare was supposed to bring. You can find Seamus Heaney's translation of it in *The Rattle Bag*, published by Faber and Faber.

'The Captain's Pearls' is what it describes: a very small poem inside a big box.

'The Sage of Kitchnapur' is not talking nonsense, although it is sometimes hard to tell.

'Spirit of the Place' contains an exercise. Part of the game is to spot what it is. The last stanza gives a hefty clue.

'The Doors' are only a few of the possible colours, and even the colours here could be seen quite differently.

'Jack's Final Riddle' . . . No comment!

If the last few poems in the book seem 'difficult', that's as it has to be, sometimes. Sometimes thoughts and feelings come together in a way that can't simply be explained, at least not without using such a conglomeration of words that you risk losing the original thrill. Really, the difference between poetry and prose isn't to do with lines and rhymes. Ordinary prose can tell you what has happened, but poetry can make it happen to you *now*.